CREE

Heather Bruegl

21st Century Junior Library

Indigenous Peoples of North America

Published in the United States of America by:

CHERRY LAKE PRESS
2395 South Huron Parkway, Suite 200, Ann Arbor, Michigan 48104
www.cherrylakepress.com

Reading Adviser: Beth Walker Gambro, MS, Ed., Reading Consultant, Yorkville, IL
Content Adviser: Aanischaaukamikw Cree Cultural Institute, Oujé-Bougoumou, Québec, Canada

Photo Credits: © Leszek Wrona/Dreamstime.com, cover, title page; © Matt Hahnewald Photography/Alamy Stock Photo, 5; © mera haval/ adapted/Shutterstock, 6; © Jon Blacker/The Canadian Press via AP, 9; © AFF/Alamy Stock Photo, 10; © Mikestockphotos/Shutterstock, 12; © jrtwynam/Shutterstock, 15; © Bryan Nature Photography/Shutterstock, 16; © awmcphee via Wikimedia Commons CC by 4.0, 19; © Danita Delimont/Alamy Stock Photo, 21

Cherry Lake Press is an imprint of Cherry Lake Publishing Group.

Library of Congress Cataloging-in-Publication Data has been filed and is available at catalog.loc.gov.

Cherry Lake Publishing would like to acknowledge the work of the Partnership for 21st Century Learning, a network of Battelle for Kids. Please visit Battelle for Kids online for more information.

Printed in the United States of America

Note from publisher: Websites change regularly, and their future contents are outside of our control. Supervise children when conducting any recommended online searches for extended learning opportunities.

About the Aanischaaukamikw Cree Cultural Institute: Special thanks and acknowledgment to the Cree staff at the Institute for providing their expertise and cultural knowledge to this project. The Aanischaaukamikw Cree Cultural Institute is Eeyou Istchee's award-winning Indigenous museum, cultural institution, and showcase of the history of the James Bay Cree that is guided by the vision and knowledge of Cree Elders. It serves as a library, archive, and teaching center. All are welcome to visit the Institute online or in person for cultural and teaching resources.

CHERRY LAKE PRESS

CONTENTS

WHO WE ARE

The Cree are the largest Indigenous group in what is now Canada. The Cree language is part of the **Algonquin** language group. The Cree sometimes call themselves *Nehiyawak* or "those who speak the same language." They may also use *Ininiwok*, or "the people." There are many **dialects** of the Cree language. That means different Cree groups may use different words. The words may also be spelled differently.

Cree peoples across Canada come together at intertribal powwows. This Cree dancer attended one in Ontario.

Create!

With an adult, explore Cree art and artists online. Print out pictures to create a collage of your favorite pieces to share.

The word *Cree* probably came from the word *Kiristinon*. French settlers recorded this word. It was borrowed from the Ojibwe. The Ojibwe used the word to refer to people living near James Bay in Canada. It was later shortened to *Cri*. It became Cree in English.

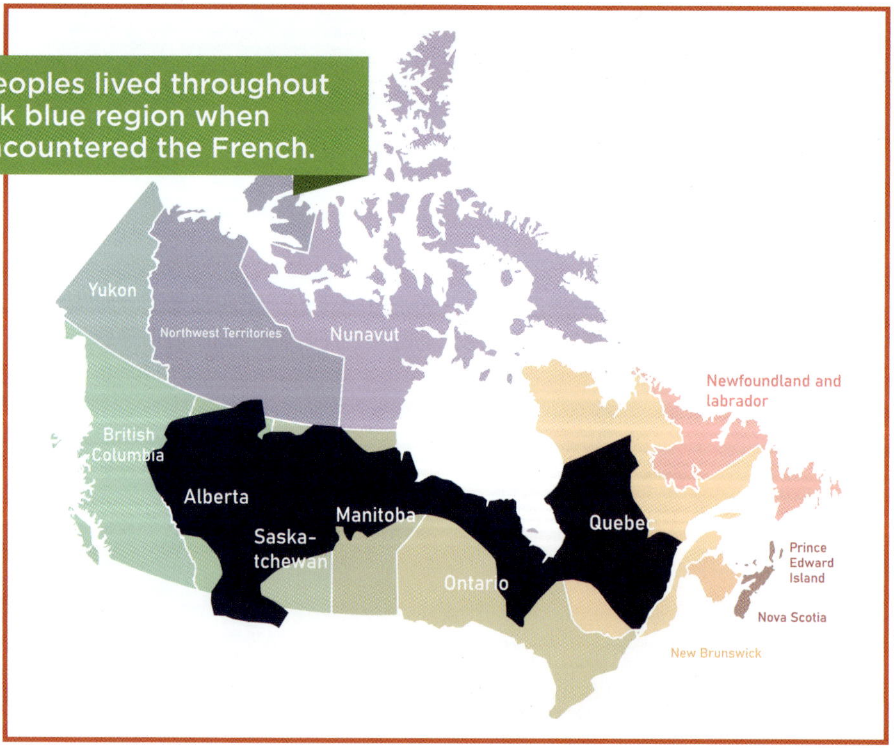

Cree peoples lived throughout the dark blue region when they encountered the French.

Think!

What does *being in community* mean to you? Think of a time you felt connected to those around you. Who was there? Why were you gathered together? How else did it make you feel?

Cree nations may also go by more local names. In Canada, Indigenous tribal nations are called **First Nations**. They were the first people to live on that land.

The Cree worldview is deeply rooted in the connection between people and nature. The Cree believe in sharing and being in community. They work to create a sense of connection and **empathy**.

OUR LIVES TODAY

The largest Cree population lives in Canada. This includes the provinces of Alberta, Quebec, Saskatchewan, Manitoba, and Ontario. Cree people live in an area larger than that of any other Canadian Indigenous group. Many Cree groups live across the country. Each has its own traditions and identity. A group of Cree people also live in the U.S. state of Montana.

Kiya Bruno is a singer and model from the Samson Cree Nation in Alberta, Canada. In 2019, at age 13, she sang Canada's national anthem in the Cree language before a Toronto Blue Jays game. It was the first time anyone had done so at that stadium.

The Cree are an important part of Canadian life. They make great contributions to the arts, science, politics, and many other areas. They bring their unique perspectives and talents to these fields. Members of Cree nations include poet Emily Riddle, hockey player Jonathan Cheechoo, and actors Michael Greyeyes and Tantoo Cardinal.

Michael Greyeyes won the 2021 Canadian Screen Award for best actor in a leading role.

Ask Questions!

Work with a librarian, teacher, or other adult. Explore how Cree life is different in Canada and the United States and how it is the same.

Cree people work to **preserve** their language and culture. They want to pass it down to future generations. They also work to protect the land. They focus on **sustainable** land use practices in areas such as mining. Cree people work with nature instead of against it. This has created a lasting relationship between the Cree and the land.

Cree lands are in many different environments, including plains and forests.

OUR ANCESTRAL LANDS

The Cree made their homes in forests and plains. Cree nations stretched across Canada and south into the Great Plains. They lived where game was plentiful and food grew well. They moved as the seasons changed. They hunted rabbits, moose, elk, and caribou in the forests. In the plains, they hunted bison. They preserved the meat by drying it over fire.

Life slowly changed after the arrival of Europeans and the beginning of colonization. Europeans set up fur trades. They built cities. They pushed the Cree into swampy areas. These areas had little game. The land did not produce food. As **colonization** grew, the Cree began to trade with Europeans. They traded for horses. They used the horses to help them hunt bison.

Fort William is in Thunder Bay, Ontario, in Canada. It was once a fur trading post. Now it is a historic site.

Traditional Cree land is rich in food sources.

Today, the Cree people live on **reserves**. These are similar to reservations in the United States. These reserves are located across their homelands in Canada. But their relationship with the land is always central. This is true of many Indigenous peoples. Hunting is still an important part of Cree culture. The Cree hunt and trap moose, caribou, rabbit, and other animals as their ancestors did.

Make a Guess!

Why do you think people carry on traditions from the past?

CARRYING TRADITIONS FORWARD

Cree traditions include ceremonies like the Sun Dance. They also include **potlatches** and **sweat lodges**. The Canadian government made these traditions illegal by passing the **Indian Act**. This was in 1876. Cree and other First Nations peoples could not practice their traditions openly. They could not own property. They could not hire lawyers. They could not leave the reserve without a pass. Later amendments changed this, but the Indian Act is still in place today. It still limits First Nations peoples.

First Nations peoples like the Cree preserved their culture. Art and music are still important in the Cree way of life. Cree women are known for their beadwork. They often create beautiful clothing and bags. Drums are sacred in Cree culture. Drum music is often linked to the Cree nation's heartbeat.

Like many Indigenous nations, the Cree worldview centers on a connection between people and nature. The Cree continue to respect nature and all living beings. Language is also essential. The Cree language is still used and taught today. It helps keep the Cree traditions moving forward.

Look!

What do you notice about how the Cree in the picture are playing the drum? How does this reflect the Cree value of being in community?

GLOSSARY

Algonquin **(al-GAHN-kwuhn)** an Indigenous language group that includes similar languages

colonization **(kah-luh-nuh-ZAY-shuhn)** the act of settling in an area and exercising control over Indigenous peoples

dialects **(DIE-uh-lekts)** variations of a shared language found in different regions or places

empathy **(EM-puh-thee)** the ability to understand the emotions or experiences of others

First Nations **(FERST NAY-shuhns)** the name given to tribal nations in Canada; it identifies these nations as the first to call Canada home

Indian Act **(IN-dee-uhn AKT)** a law in Canada that encouraged Indigenous nations to forget their Indigenous ways and banned the practice of traditional religions

potlatches **(PAHT-latch-uhz)** Indigenous gift-giving feasts, typically lasting multiple days and marked by distributing or destroying wealth

preserve **(prih-ZERV)** to protect and keep safe from harm

reserves **(rih-ZERVZ)** legally designated areas of land for Indigenous peoples in Canada

sustainable **(suh-STAY-nuh-buhl)** describing a method of using a resource that does not use up or damage it

sweat lodges **(SWET LAH-juz)** ceremonial buildings built to trap the heat of a central fire causing those inside to sweat; ceremonial places used for purification and cleansing rituals

FIND OUT MORE

Books

Simpson, Tonya. *Forever Our Home / kâkikê kîkinaw*. Custer, WA: Orca Book Publishers, 2023.

Sorell, Traci. *We Are Grateful: Otsaliheliga*. Watertown, MA: Charlesbridge, 2021.

Sorell, Traci. *We Are Still Here! Native American Truths Everyone Should Know*. Watertown, MA: Charlesbridge, 2021.

Online

With an adult, explore more online with these suggested searches.

- "All about Cree Culture, Language and Traditions," The Gift of Language and Culture
- "Cree," The Canadian Encyclopedia

Say Hello!

Wachiye (WAA-chee-yeh) and *kweih* (KWAY) are Cree for "hello."
Tanisi (TAHN-say) is another way of saying "Hello, how are you?"

INDEX

ABOUT THE AUTHOR

Heather Bruegl, a member of the Oneida Nation of Wisconsin/Stockbridge-Munsee, is a Madonna University graduate with a Master of Arts in U.S. History. She is a public historian and decolonial educator, and her Munsee name is Kiishookunkwe, which means "Sunflower in Full Bloom." Heather frequently travels to present on Indigenous history, policy, and activism, bringing her deep knowledge and personal connection to the subject.